I AM ME

ADULT

Lynn Given

Copyright 2019 by Lynn Given

The book author retains sole copyright to her contributions to this book. Published 2019. Printed in the United States of America.
All rights reserved.

No portion of this book may be reproduced, stored in a retrieval system, or transmitted in any form or by any means – electronic, mechanical, photocopy, recording, scanning, or other – except for brief quotations in critical reviews or articles, without the prior written permission of the author.

Publisher's Cataloging-in-Publication data
Names: Given, Lynn, author.
Title: I Am Me - Adults / Lynn Given.
Description: First trade paperback original edition. | Parker [Colorado] : Lynn Given, 2019.
Identifiers: ISBN 978-1-950647-11-8
Subjects: LCSH: Affirmations.
BISAC: SELF-HELP / Affirmations.
Classification: LCC 637.S4 | DDC 158.1–dc22

---

lynngiven.com

Published by BookCrafters, Parker, Colorado.

Dedication

This book is dedicated to my two beautiful sons, Jake and Justin. I must confess that they are, without a doubt, the greatest source of inspiration behind every word I wrote in this book. They helped me become the best that I can be.

They have brought love and joy into my life since the day they were born, and they will illuminate my life forever. I am grateful to have two beautiful children to share my life and accomplishments with for many years to come. The only hope that I have left is that I can inspire them with this book to the same extent that they have done for me.

I also want to say a special thank you to my husband Jamie for all the love and support he has given me during our journey together. None of this would have been possible without him.

Finally, I wish to thank everyone who has been part of the writing, editing, and publishing process of this book.

Introduction

There is nobody else like you and you should be proud of yourself. We are all unique in our own way, and by accepting your uniqueness you can achieve everything you want in life. Once you realize that your differences make you stand out from the others, you will be able to walk your own path in life with greater ease and obtain greater success from it.

The main goal of this book is to inspire you to create a better version of yourself. Moreover, this book will help you identify how you are unique and exceptional. It is my personal hope that your optimism will shine through as you read this - whether it's in a single section or the entire work. Every word should inspire you to be grateful for what is happening in your life by appreciating the small moments and finding happiness in little details that surround you.

You will also learn about the great virtue that is patience. Having this attribute will help you understand the people around you so you will be able to offer them a helping hand or be an inspiration in their lives.

There's nothing more uplifting than knowing that others are able to recognize what you have to give.

But remember—there is always room for improvement. Above all, this is what will help you be the best version of yourself. You have to be mindful of your own experience of the world and how that can vary wildly from one perspective to the next. Sometimes, putting the needs of others before your own is what it takes to obtain that mindfulness. There's great power in recognizing that others might be in need of your support, love, and understanding.

I hope this book resonates with you. For it is here that you may find the values and inspiration that will guide you through the rest of your life.

Remember to read each statement with deep feeling and truly believe!

I am Dependable

I am Compassionate

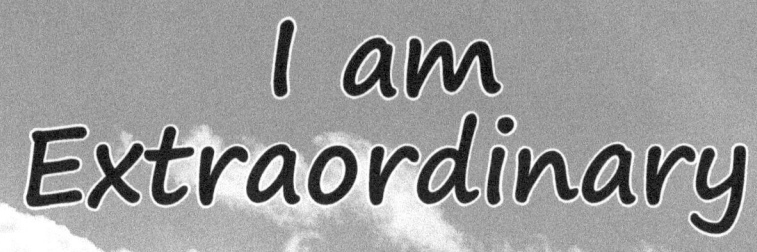

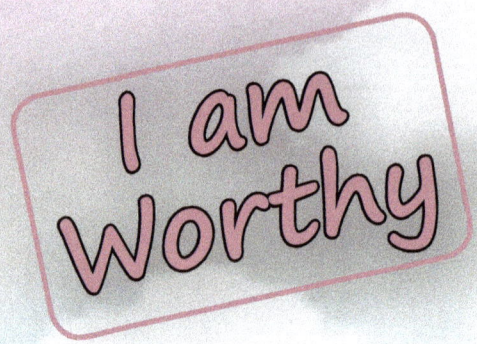

I am Wonderful

I am FREE

I am Determined

Thank you

I am Thankful

I am An Action Taker

I am
Focused

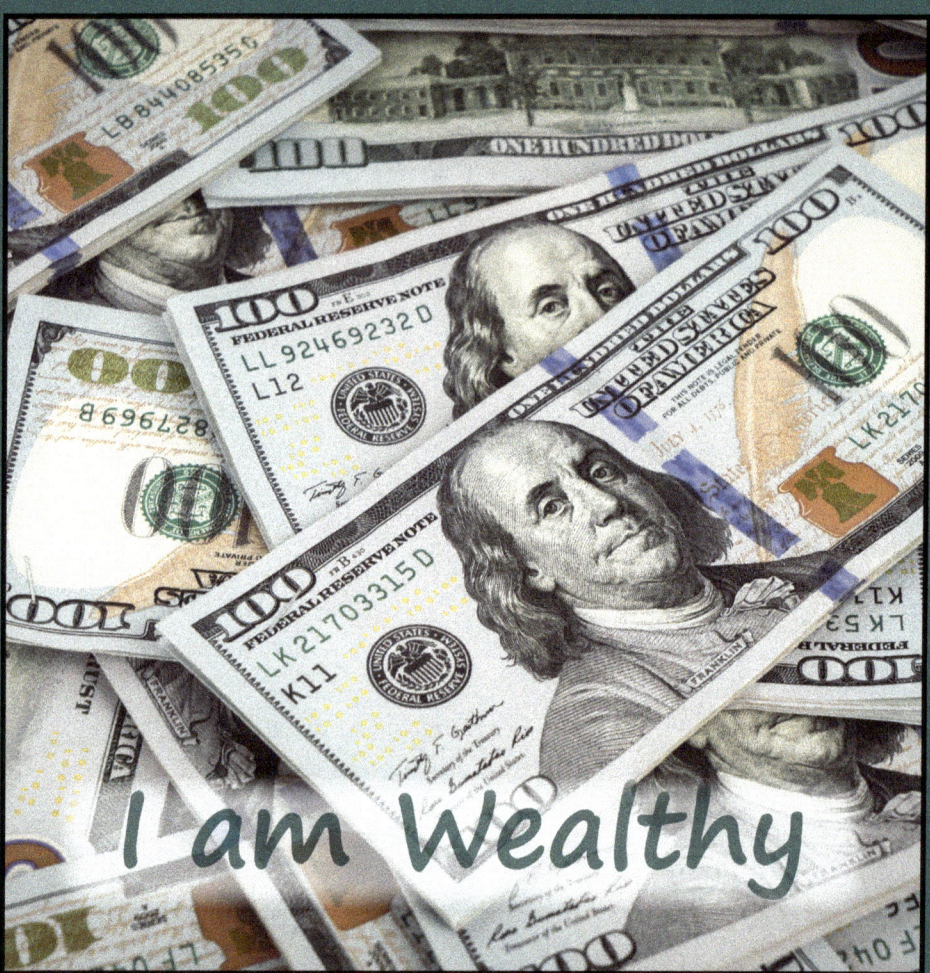

I am _____

_____

_____

_____

_____

_____

_____

_____

_____

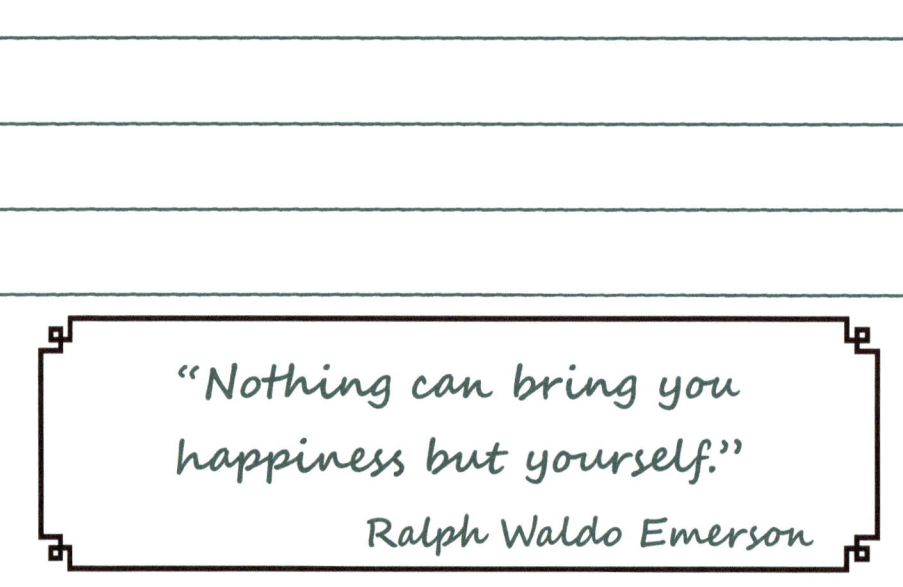

"Nothing can bring you happiness but yourself."
Ralph Waldo Emerson

Namasté